Lorem ipsum dolor sit consectetur adipisicing elit, eiusmod tempor incididu labore et dolore magna **aliq enim ad minim veniam, nostrud exercitation ulb laboris nisi ut aliquip commodo consequat. Duis irure dolor in reprehende voluptate** *velit esse cillum a eu fugiat nulla pariatur. Exc sint occaecat cupidatat proident, sunt in culpa qui deserunt mollit anim i laborum.*

5% 50% 75% 100% 5% 10% 25% 50% 75% 100%

13   14   15   16   17

D0018375

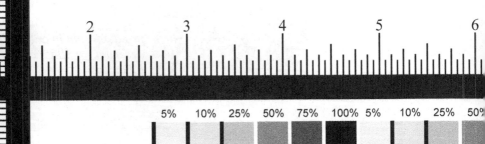

5% 10% 25% 50% 75% 100% 5% 10% 25% 50%

Lorem ipsum dolor sit amet, consectetur adipisicing elit, sed do eiusmod tempor incididunt ut labore et dolore magna **aliqua. Ut enim ad minim veniam, quis nostrud exercitation ullamco laboris nisi ut aliquip ex ea commodo consequat. Duis aute irure dolor in reprehenderit in voluptate** *velit esse cillum dolore eu fugiat nulla pariatur. Excepteur sint occaecat cupidatat non proident, sunt in culpa qui officia deserunt mollit anim id est laborum.*

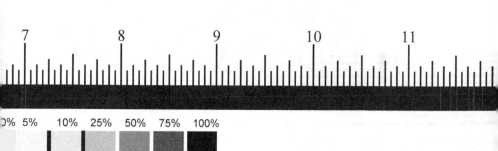

7　　　　　8　　　　　9　　　　10　　　　11

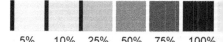

Lorem ipsum dolor sit amet, consectetur adipisicing elit, sed do eiusmod tempor incididunt ut labore et dolore magna **aliqua. Ut enim ad minim veniam, quis nostrud exercitation ullamco laboris nisi ut aliquip ex ea commodo consequat. Duis aute irure dolor in reprehenderit in voluptate** *velit esse cillum dolore eu fugiat nulla pariatur. Excepteur sint occaecat cupidatat non proident, sunt in culpa qui officia deserunt mollit anim id est laborum.*

Lorem ipsum dolor sit amet, consectetur adipisicing elit, sed do eiusmod tempor incididunt ut labore et dolore magna **aliqua. Ut enim ad minim veniam, quis nostrud exercitation ullamco laboris nisi ut aliquip ex ea commodo consequat. Duis aute irure dolor in reprehenderit in voluptate** *velit esse cillum dolore eu fugiat nulla pariatur. Excepteur sint occaecat cupidatat non proident, sunt in culpa qui officia deserunt mollit anim id est laborum.*

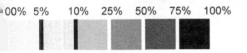

00% 5%   10%   25%   50%   75%   100%

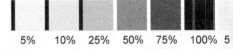

5%   10%   25%   50%   75%   100% 5

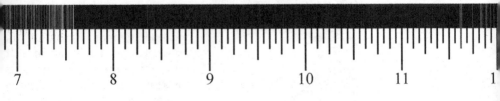

7   8   9   10   11   1

Lorem ipsum dolor sit
consectetur adipisicing elit,
eiusmod tempor incididu
labore et dolore magna **aliq**
enim ad minim veniam,
nostrud exercitation ull
laboris nisi ut aliquip
commodo consequat. Dui
irure dolor in reprehende
voluptate *velit esse cillum*
eu fugiat nulla pariatur. Exc
sint occaecat cupidatat
proident, sunt in culpa qui
deserunt mollit anim i
laborum.

5% 10% 25% 50% 75% 100% 5%

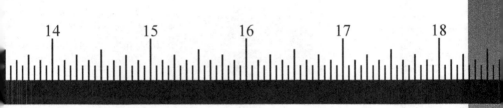

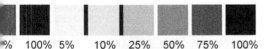

% 100% 5% 10% 25% 50% 75% 100%

Lorem ipsum dolor sit amet, consectetur adipisicing elit, sed do eiusmod tempor incididunt ut labore et dolore magna **aliqua. Ut enim ad minim veniam, quis nostrud exercitation ullamco laboris nisi ut aliquip ex ea commodo consequat. Duis aute irure dolor in reprehenderit in voluptate** *velit esse cillum dolore eu fugiat nulla pariatur. Excepteur sint occaecat cupidatat non proident, sunt in culpa qui officia deserunt mollit anim id est laborum.*

Approaching Winter

LOUISIANA STATE UNIVERSITY PRESS   BATON ROUGE

Approaching Winter

POEMS

FLOYD SKLOOT

Published by Louisiana State University Press
Copyright © 2015 by Floyd Skloot
All rights reserved
Manufactured in the United States of America
LSU Press Paperback Original
First printing

Designer: Mandy McDonald Scallan | *Typeface:* Minion Pro | *Printer and binder:* LSI

These poems were previously published in the following journals: *Acumen* (England): "Late"; *Bellevue Literary Review:* "Ahihi Bay"; *Boulevard:* "Crying over 'Scarlet Ribbons,'" "First Night in London, 2012," "Late May in Zuheros, Andalucía," and "Traumatic Brain Injury"; *Cerise Press* (online): "Lost in the Memory Palace"; *Florida Review:* "Signs" and "Turning Sixty-Five"; *Franklin & Marshall Alumni Arts Review:* "Laughter and Music" and "Signs"; *Galway Review* (Ireland): "Day's End"; *Hollins Critic:* "Sunday in Queens, 1952"; *Hopkins Review:* "Barrier Island," "Handspun," "Returning Home," and "Today"; *Hudson Review:* "Samuel Beckett Throws Out the First Pitch"; *Literature and Belief:* "Dylan Thomas at Sundown, November 9, 1953"; *Margie:* "Dylan Thomas at Sundown, November 9, 1953"; *Memoir Journal:* "Laughter and Music"; *The Moth* (Ireland): "Laughter and Music" and "Sightings"; *New Welsh Review* (Wales): "At the Fitness Center"; *New World Writing* (formerly *Mississippi Review Online* and *BLIP* online): "Approaching Winter" and "Dream of a Childhood"; *Notre Dame Review:* "Lost in the Memory Palace"; *Plume* (online): "Breathing Room," "Handel in London, 1741," "Late," "In Memory," and "Thomas Hardy in the Dorset County Museum"; *Poem Magazine* (England): "Dylan Thomas at Sundown, November 9, 1953" and "In Memory"; *Poetry Daily* (online): "Ahihi Bay" and "The Movie Maker"; *Poetry Ireland Review:* "Approaching Winter" and "Lost in the Memory Palace"; *Prairie Schooner:* "Castaway," "My Grandfather's Final Day in the Old Country, 1892," "Osprey Rhapsody," and "Youth"; *The Sewanee Review:* "Fender's Blue," "The Hammer Throw," and "The Movie Maker"; *Southern Poetry Review:* "Sightings"; *The Southern Review:* "Jet Lag in La Mancha" and "October 30, 1938"; *Stinging Fly* (Ireland): "Breathing Room," "October 30, 1938," and "Today"; *Tiferet:* "Day's End" and "Sturgeon Season"; *Valparaiso Poetry Review* (online): "Labor Day Party in Brooklyn, 1953"; *Zyzzyva:* "At the Fitness Center" and "Spanish Edition."

I am grateful for the help of my wife, Beverly Hallberg, as the first reader of these poems, and for the comments from Ron Slate, my friend of nearly forty years.

Library of Congress Cataloging-in-Publication Data

Skloot, Floyd.
  [Poems. Selections]
  Approaching winter : poems / Floyd Skloot.
     pages ; cm
  ISBN 978-0-8071-6017-6 (pbk. : alk. paper) — ISBN 978-0-8071-6018-3 (epub) — ISBN 978-0-8071-6019-0 (pdf) — ISBN 978-0-8071-6020-6 (mobi)
  I. Title.
  PS3569.K577A6 2016
  811'.54—dc23
                                                                    2014049784

For my daughter Rebecca
with love and gratitude

CONTENTS

I

My Grandfather's Final Day in the Old Country, 1892

Last night soldiers on horseback circled
the house of worship. He saw the blazing
roof cave in, heard screams, felt heat curl
around his body, but thought it all a crazy
dream. Would God let His own house be consumed
in fire? Now charred wood and ash coat the mud,
the lungs, lingering in air near the ruined
synagogue. Glass shards catch the morning sun.
God allows the holy ark to burn? At twelve
he already knows what the Rabbi would say
to that question, if the Rabbi were still alive:
Evidently, my child. This is the day
he should be walking his brother to school
for the first time, but the school is cinder
and thin spirals of smoke. If it were true,
as the Rabbi taught, that God's fire bore
the light from which the universe was formed,
could it be that fire was not such a bad thing?
What is God saying when He brings harm
to bear upon people gathered to sing
His praises, and then lets the very place
where they sing dissolve in flame? He has seen
what he came to see, so he turns to face
the river one last time, closes his eyes, breathes
in the unfamiliar air, and tries to pray.

October 30, 1938

The night Martians landed in New Jersey
my father was just across the Hudson River
asking for my mother's hand in marriage.
My grandfather is supposed to have said
You can have all of her. Then they drank
a schnapps, toasting life, toasting my mother
pacing in another room, and sat on the sofa
listening to chaos rising from the street.

It was a Sunday, getting late, getting dark,
and all my father could think about was
why such traffic? He had to be awake
by four, open his market by five, it was
already late to be driving back to Brooklyn.

As he stood, someone cried out on the fire
escape above. A radio crackled with static
as the wind shifted and rose, making scraps
of newspaper drift past the window.
He thought about all my mother wanted—
the honeymoon in Cuba, aproned maid,
ritzy apartment on a top floor, his thick
hands washed clean of blood *even
under the fingernails* before he ever
entered their home—and knew himself to be
in an alien world. But he was thirty,
she was twenty-eight, and it was time.

He walked out into the cold and saw
on a stoop across the street a woman
wearing ragged slippers and a mink stole
kneeling in prayer as the crowd rushed east.
One carried a canary in its cage.

A man grabbed my father's arm. *It's happening*
right now! Tears streaked the man's face
as he said *They've got heat rays and poison*
gas. You'll never make it and my father thought
But I just did. His car was surrounded,
a couple in evening wear draped across
its hood, a child perched on its rear bumper
holding a stuffed platypus. *The Martians*
are big as skyscrapers and fast as express
trains. Jersey's gone. They're coming this way.

My father unlocked the door and looked
back a moment to see my mother framed
in her window, face turned away from him
as she watched her neighbors flowing
out of sight. He knew it was going to take
all night to find his slow way home.

Laughter and Music

I know he must have been able to laugh.
There's a picture from the days before
photoshop in which he's holding a gaff
like a harpoon and standing on some shore
amid buckets filled with mussels and clams.
His head is arched back, eyes gleaming, mouth wide
with delight. So I have proof. There's a chance
he really told a Yiddish joke that one night
I recall, and I heard he played the fiddle.
My aunt, when he died fifty years ago
this month, told me—after dinner in the middle
of our week of mourning—that he loved mambo
before he met my mother. So I know
he could shake his hips, manage kick and flick,
lose himself in laughter and music,
do La Cucaracha, do quick-quick-slow.

The Movie Maker

My father was a haphazard home
movie maker. He left the camera
running in its case, shot directly
into sunlight, lost scenes in shadow.
His hands shook or jerked the lens back
and forth across the family huddled
on a bluff. He captured nothing
but my brother's white buck shoes
as they moved through clipped grass,
me half-headed on an Adirondack chair.
I used to think it meant he could not bear
to see us as we were. Specializing in
double exposure, he superimposed
a summer vacation in upstate New York
over a Sunday morning of sledding
in Prospect Park, or a gleaming Seder
table over a morning visit to the cemetery,
headstones unsteady in what may have
been autumn rain. When we packed
to move, I found a bag of undeveloped
reels stashed in the attic and dated
a month before he died. Knowing what
to expect from my parents' last trip
together did not prepare me for
the sight of cars on the Amalfi Drive
passing through the Coliseum
in the heart of Rome, clouds adrift
above a ramshackle hotel roof, or my
mother frowning while he tried to bring
her into focus on the Spanish Steps,
my last chance to see as he did.

Lost in the Memory Palace

I found my brother in the attic
of the memory palace
hunched over our old Silvertone
under rafters where late afternoon
light streamed through a gable vent.
His face wavered in a haze of dust.
Before I could speak he looked
up and raised a finger to his lips.
The sound of wind was the soft
southern voice of Red Barber
broadcasting a Dodgers game.
Ol' Duke's easy as a bank of fog.

It wasn't supposed to work
like this. I should know where I've put
people to find them in a heartbeat:
Father buried long ago in the cellar,
mother at the piano in the parlor,
brother eating Velveeta before
the open fridge. But then
just this morning—I think it was
this morning—my father stumbled out
of the library where he would never
be found. He had a book in hand,
the title concealed by his fingers,
and was smiling in a way I never saw
him smile before. I almost missed him,
thinking the short man with the bald
spot gleaming as he turned must be me.

I don't remember my brother
doing anything like that scene in the attic.
No secret corners of rooms, no hunching
over radios, no hushed moments I recall.
He filled his spaces, and was gone
whenever I couldn't hear or see him.

And now I don't know where
my mother is because she seems to be
everywhere at once. I can hear her
in the parlor playing the opening chords
of "Bewitched, Bothered and Bewildered,"
but instead of singing she screams
from the living room where a smudged
fingerprint has been found on a low
credenza we never owned.

She also waits at the bottom of the ladder
I used to climb into the attic, arms
akimbo, smoke from her Chesterfield
drifting up to mingle with the dust.

Dream of a Childhood

Childhood was a raft drifting across
the Pacific. It was sometimes a shiny yellow
Geiger counter and sometimes the polio
vaccine at last, which meant you could swim
again in public pools. Childhood was a fat
stack of Green Stamp books on a cloverleaf
table in the foyer. It was coonskin caps
on boys from Brooklyn, then the end of *Wait
Till Next Year.* All you had to do was dream.

Waking to "Yakety Yak" on the radio,
moving so fast no one heard it but you,
childhood was don't turn on the lights,
tiptoe around the kitchen so your mother
continued sleeping. It was a week's worth
of hard-boiled eggs peeled and waiting
in the refrigerator. It was your mother's dream
of no mess, no trace, no mornings to endure.

Childhood was grade school beside a Nike
missile base on the bay side of a barrier
island. It was duck-and-cover drills in home
room. Teachers had ham radios and decals
from all forty-eight states, foreign coins
in a plate on the desk. One called you Dream
Boat when you gazed out the winter window
and began to doze. Teachers ate lunches
in a secret room stacked with Tupperware
and recalled honeymoons dancing in Havana.

Brothers drove Tango Red Chryslers
to land's-end and back, over and over.
You dreamed yours would be Parisian Blue
and go twice as fast as his. Sisters had packs
of Old Gold cigarettes you saw dancing in ads
on television. Friends' mothers wore frilled
aprons. They carried platters of standing
rib roast, fixed molded domes of lemon Jell-o
mixed with tomato sauce and topped by loops
of mayonnaise. Fathers rose in the dark
and vanished till the dark returned them
ready for sleep, ready for their own dreaming.

Sunday in Queens, 1952

My father's black Buick brought the sun down
all around us. We inched up the Van Wyck,
windows shut because Mother wore a crown
of hair breeze might unseat. She was sick
and tired of my complaints. I saw the air
throb above our hood. Oceans could boil, land
soften till it oozed with mud, heavens glare
away all cloud, and I knew for a fact sand
without the wash of storm tides had become pure
heat in the year since I last walked through it
myself. This was late June and I was sure
the world was going up in smoke. Minute
by minute as we crawled through the clogged heart
of Queens, I waited for the blaze to start.

Labor Day Party in Brooklyn, 1953

Through a haze of words and bursts
of laughter, I watch solid cherry
Parsons tables float as though
balanced on wings. Despite the heat,
Mother wears her sable stole.
She weaves among the dancers,
gripping ice in silver tongs,
finding golden drinks to freshen.
Father has all the answers tonight,
has aces high, has licked his jinx
for good. There is so much noise
the street sounds fit right in,
and such sparkling the glimmer
of streetlights through torn screens
only adorns the party's edges.
This night-world shimmers with late
summer laughter, its skin pure
sound like the sigh that follows song,
strange as parents who kiss
when they pass. Our guests move
from light to shadow and back.

Breathing Room

Not every week,
but sometimes one night
a month, the four of us
were in the same room
and there would be
not quite peace,
not even truce,
but a time that felt like slow
release of the family's held
breath, and I could feel
my heart begin to slow,
not enough to clear my head
but enough to remind me
not to move quickly,
not to speak, not even
to look up and risk
meeting someone's eyes.

Castaway

Long Beach, N.Y., 1957

I told myself that rescue could come soon.
The island was not far from shipping lanes
and at all hours of the day I saw planes
overhead. I would be found in late June

when the weather was warmer, or in fall
because people always want one more long
journey before winter. There was a song
I made up to sing at night that named all

the secret places that were left behind.
My parents would explain why we had moved
here from the city but that only proved
what I suspected: they had lost their minds.

It was up to me to save us. The dunes
would swell and shrink with the seasons, the tide
rise and fall. At the beach, time could not hide.
I told myself that rescue would come soon.

Late

The last time my father returned from work
there was just enough daylight left for me
to watch his shadow follow on the street.
I was coming home from the beach to meet
him as usual and I can still see
the way he stopped for breath under an arc
of maple limbs, the way he looked around
without noticing I was there behind
him on the rise. Sand rode a sea breeze thick
with the familiar scent of brine and fish.
Soon he would move again. He would climb
the stairs, laughing gulls would still be the sound
of summer sun, I would still be fourteen
and have no reason to recall that scene.

In Memory

November 11, 1961

I remember the night my father died
wind-blown snow raged at my bedroom window.
But now I read online that it was dry
and calm all week. I can still see in slow
motion the way my brother turned his back,
took off his glasses, and cried as he heard
the news over the phone. I see the black
frames flicker with firelight and hear the word
dead for myself as it leaks from his ear,
though now I can see in a photograph
that his frames from those days were clear.
I would even swear that I heard him laugh
then, a hacking sound that I keep inside,
forgotten till the night my brother died.

Traumatic Brain Injury

Long Beach, N.Y., October 1962

In the parking lot I can hear
the thin staccato crack and snap
of snare drums carried from behind
the Hall of Music on a swirl
of lake winds. As a pea whistle
stops and restarts the drum line,
I listen for trumpets and horns,
cheering voices, and my own
whispered breath. Then I am back
fifty years, and wind now laced
with sand carries the same brittle
rapping. I run onto a field
wet with spray and scoured by salt,
then stand alone near the end zone
awaiting the opening kick.
My helmet's ear holes fuse the thump
of breath and drums as the world
slows to a football tumbling through
morning glare and into my arms.
I rush toward the oncoming tacklers.

The Hammer Throw

At the edge of a winter-blunted dune,
he takes a deep breath and grows still.
Then he flexes his knees, rocks his hips,
tightens his grip, and begins to spin
circles through sparkles of sunlight
and flickering shadow as he practices
turning faster and faster, swinging
the ball-and-chain above his head.
My childhood friend is alive again,
heaving the hammer at the tideline.
And I am with him, dodging spume,
marking the flight until the hammer
lands in a burst of sand and I can
carry it back for one last throw.

Youth

I stand in the foreground, nine
or ten years old, stiff in a dark
suit, shirt buttoned to the throat,
handkerchief in my breast pocket,
shoulder gripped by my mother.
Her expression says *take*
the goddamn picture NOW.
My expression is turned
wholly inward as I listen to
a voice urging me to keep
still, breathe later.
I have dozens of photos
in which my fingers are this
rigid, my eyes this
blackened by blows from my
mother's hands. A late
morning breeze lifts
the pale green tips
of her silken scarf.
Sunlight catches the heavy
globes of her earrings
and soft white gloves
dangling from her closed fist.

II

Handspun

My wife sits in her swivel chair
ringed by skeins of multicolored yarn
that will become the summer sweater
she has imagined since September.
Her hand rests on the spinning wheel
and her foot pauses on the pedals
as she gazes out into the swollen river.
Light larking between wind and current
will be in this sweater. So will a shade
of red she saw when the sun went down.
When she is at her wheel, time moves
like the tune I almost recognize now
that she begins to hum it, a lulling
melody born from the draft of fiber,
clack of spindle and bobbin, soft
breath as the rhythm takes hold.

Approaching Winter

Late afternoons when the sun slips behind
the hills I like to sit by my window
facing east and watch shadows capture
the river. Cormorants skim the surface
as though preying on the edge of light
and yellow tugboats nudge gravel barges
into the spreading dark. Once I saw a siege
of herons packed onto the trunk of a young
ash tree swirling in current after a storm.
Now a kayak gliding downstream vanishes
as it follows the bank's curve below me.
In a few months I'll be sixty-five.

Lately, at this time of day, I'm not
always sure where the borders of sleep
might be. Memory ebbs and floods as I try
not to doze. My infant daughter's voice
is somewhere within the calls of circling
eagles though she is two thousand miles
away, a grown woman at work on a book
in her own attic aerie. My father smiles
and dives into a pool where he is about
to die, but surfaces in front of me here,
playful as an otter in these waters.
My wife stands near me at her easel
breaking the river into bold vectors
of color. Her sweet alto rises
with the tune flowing into her ears.

As I stare, a shift in wind transforms
the midriver pattern into prairie
grass, into ice losing hold of itself,
then into Hemingway on a paddleboard
waving at me. He wants me to move,
I think, wants to lure me out of the house
and onto the fishing boat he must command,
anchored near the pilings where a dock
used to be. Across the river, at the tip
of Ross Island where cottonwoods are still
holding their leaves, an overturned stump
can only be Gertrude Stein signaling
with a flutter of arms that she expects
to join us. We'll need to avoid Moses
in his cradle now drifting close to shore
disguised as the bole of a white oak.

The room has grown cold. When my wife lights
the fire behind me, the window fills
with its flickering glow. It's a kind of smile
that eases me from the chair, and she's there
with me, both ready for the night to come.

Crying over "Scarlet Ribbons"

I remember my daughter wanted pink
plastic barrettes for her hair. One on each
side of her forehead. They are there, I think,
in this blurred photo of her on a beach
somewhere in Washington, and in this one,
sitting on a ceramic pirate's lap
at a zoo in Madison, Wisconsin.
I swear they are under her sailor cap
here as she drives a tiny British race car
in Tomorrowland. On a camping trip
through North Dakota, one beloved star-
shaped barrette was lost when I failed to clip
it properly in place. We backtracked all
the way to Grand Forks in search of new
pink stars. And here she stands in early fall,
hair grown longer now, light finding the two
barrettes we bought at an old drugstore just
as the day and our hopes seemed lost.

At the Fitness Center

Framed by a picture window,
two old men climbing stairs to nowhere
watch the river flow.
As though gliding on air
beside
them, a woman with violet hair,
wires dangling from her ears,
keeps her eyes shut tight
and sings out of tune while she strides
on the elliptical machine
next to mine.
A husband and wife jog in place
on treadmills side-by-side,
keeping pace
with each other and trying to plan
the next two
nights' dinners though they can
barely speak. A teen
with his cap on backwards cycles through
a mountain pass
as his girlfriend screams
and kickboxes behind shaded glass.

Sturgeon Season

They have been there since dawn,
their boats side-by-side midriver,
lines cast downstream into the edge
of deep water, sipping coffee as light
seeps through naked branches of ash
and cottonwood. Now from shadows
of limbs and swirling current a sea lion
slithers among their orange anchor
buoys and dives. The water,
already roiled brown and swollen
by rain, is so cold it seems to crack
when a cormorant skims the surface
before rising toward its island nest.

Signs

The river swells with melted mountain snow.
Soon driftwood spinning in the current's grip
begins to gather like a ghostly grove
high on the island's dwindling shore. Winter
has not let go of the nights, but the trees
are in leaf near the western bank and great
blue heron hunt the shallows. No soft breeze,
no long days of cloudless skies or a late
afternoon hint of summer on its way.
Just a feeling of mildness in the air,
and some heavy rain, and not every day.
To the north there may be less space where
that tugboat passes underneath the bridge.
South in this light the river looks like sludge.

Osprey Rhapsody

Hunched on the boom
of a shipbuilder's crane,
an osprey watches
her chick flap and fall
back into their nest
atop a light pole
a hundred yards east.
Mexico beckons
in fading summer
light. On the river,
two dragonboats pass
near shore, the callers'
shrill voices mingling
with the birds' cries now
joined by the circling
father, wings arched, fish
dangling from his talons.
Facing the light pole
near the water's edge,
a man plays stand-up
bass with his eyes closed,
head tilting in time
to the melody.
The chick calms, softened
chirps finding spaces
within the music
and dimming voices,
head barely visible
above the nest's rim.

Fender's Blue

The evening distance is a shade of blue
I have not seen before. Cottonwood trees
along the riverbank have lost their leaves
like this every year and let light through
with the same stirring of wind in their tops.
The sky reminds me of the ospreys' cries
again, their frenzied parting shriek that stops
me in my tracks year after year and stays
in the dense dark air, refusing to fade.
But this year the river and clouds call
to mind the heron's plumage in full molt,
ragged and gray across the current. Bold
black and white soars only where sight
is edged with reflection by the coming night.
It feels as though I have gotten too old
for the hues I can remember. This fall
those stars may be the last Fender's blue
butterflies anyone will see around here.

Cleanup Project

They have been out there for two years now
working to cap and contain the shipbuilder's
waste. Some nights wind catches in the mast
and jib of the crane parked by the riverbank
or frees a puff of dust from a bulldozer's bucket.
Some nights passing clouds make the huddled
backhoes and excavators seem to breathe
in the moonlight. A dump truck half-filled
with rubble sits on steel plates, tires caked
with toxic mud. At seven they all shriek
awake and pass between us and the glassy
waters where a trio of sculls sweeps upstream.

III

Handel in London, 1741

Wedged in a chair near the open window,
Handel gasps and wheezes as he takes in
the August air, fanning himself with a sheaf
of jumbled scripture Jennens gave to him.

He knows the time has come to turn away
from text, move beyond thoughts of prophecy,
sacrifice, or resurrection, and find his way
to the wracked, seething place where words

stop and music always lurks. Where God's
glory awaits release. He has not been well.
Stroke, melancholy, the weight of work.
He has begun to imagine an end, the terror

of unending silence. Not sure he could rise
from the chair if he wanted to, he closes
his eyes and imagines Ireland, the viceroy's
invitation, the sea breeze ahead. He dozes

a moment, then starts because all those old
scraps he has been hearing, brief passages
from operas he wrote long ago, from Italian
duets, songs for castrato, are returning,

insisting he make use of them, clear his mind
for fresh melodies. He feels his heart race,
the familiar frenzy beginning to bring
him close to the face of God. *Hallelujah.*

Dylan Thomas at Sundown, November 9, 1953

Dylan Thomas drifts above the sea,
savoring the sundown light of memory.
Waves lap the shingle. He feels nothing
beneath his empty body and decides
he must be riding a froth of cloud.

What surprises him most is the pure
silence within and without. It folds
over itself like the breakers below.
He thought there would be music
at the end, something like the melody
of starburst, and singing, flowing lyrics
in a language known only to angels.
He thought there would be nothing
like time, nothing like this sense of loss.

Afloat on dead air, he sees himself
sprint across hay fields. Thirty years
gone in the blink of an eye. He is far
ahead of the children chasing with voices
fading. Not even the desperate fox
can keep pace as the wild boy flashes by.
He always knew this would be the moment
remembered forever. Life was one mad
dash to a finish line hidden at land's-end,
a quick lick. He would be breathless
at the end, down on his knees as if in prayer,
but finally able to slow his heart, his mind,
there at the darkening ocean's edge.

Samuel Beckett Throws Out the First Pitch

Ebbets Field, Brooklyn, August 1957

The lanky lefty standing on the first-base
side of the mound flips the ball from hand
to hand and studies the distance between
late afternoon shadow and evening light.

No one is sure who he is. The former cricket
bowler S. B. Beckett, his letter had said.
Irish, long retired from the sport, and that
was good enough for the O'Malley family
to welcome him in the melancholy dog
days of their Dodgers' last season in Brooklyn.

Friends imagine him in London or Paris,
maybe somewhere in Normandy, out of touch,
at work on a play. But he imagines himself
in a place where play as he'd known it
at last becomes strange enough for joy.
He has dressed in white from shoes to jumper.

Under his fierce stare home plate transforms
itself into a wicket right before the bored
eyes of Roy Campanella settling into a crouch
and expecting a soft lob from an old man
about to vanish from sight. Then the ball
in Beckett's huge hand turns red as he molds
his fingers against its crease. He squares up.

All around him are the ruins of a great
stadium and he sees what will become of it,
smashed to rubble and broken memory,
names echoing in thickened air. Now ghosts
drift in a warp of time like the voices
of this sparse crowd paying no attention
as Beckett sinks deeper into himself.

He calls to mind the form of a perfect pitch,
the spin ball he will unleash from a windmilling
arm, the held breath filled with nothing but his own
heartbeat, a silent moment before action
that he never wants to end. Then, stifling a cry,
he begins to run straight toward home.

Thomas Hardy in the Dorset County Museum

Turned sideways in a desk chair,
elbow perched on its top rail,
the life-size cardboard Thomas Hardy
looks wary. Even when no one is here
Hardy sits tight, certain something
must take him from happy solitude.
Work is everywhere now, a poem's
lines whirling in a figure-eight above
his head, chapter one of a novel
looming behind him, rough drafts
of letters under glass at his knee.
Apologizing, knowing he never liked
being touched, I drape my arm over
his shoulder as my wife takes our picture.
He is much younger than I am,
not the sage Hardy with wizened face,
wispy hair and waxed mustache tips.
His beard is darker, thicker, his hair
shorter, but the matching domes
of our foreheads are enough to
let me feel what I have come all
this way to feel. It is time to move on
to the place where he was born.

Ahihi Bay

for Beverly

So far this morning has been cool and gray
but as she walks backward into the sea,
adjusting her snorkel and mask, sunlight
appears over Haleakalā's cone
to show the water all around her blue.
Teardrop butterfly and unicornfish
wait for her, saddle wrasse and leatherback,
yellow tang and spotted puffer. She sinks
into the surf and drifts above antler
coral and long-spined urchins where a green
sea turtle swam beside her yesterday.
The breeze dies down. From where I stand
on black lava outcroppings she is still,
though I know her arms and legs are moving
in the world of reef triggerfish and fire
dartfish. She rises and falls as the waves
seem to pass through her, turning her almost
imperceptibly toward the horizon.

Jet Lag in La Mancha

The sky darkened and sagged as we drove
south through the plains of La Mancha,
heading for an inn in Andalucía. The storm
found us just before Madridejos. We slowed
in the heavy rain, our Citroën rattled by gusts,
feeling as though we were going nowhere,
losing touch with time. But when light returned
the flat land around us was central Kansas,
sunflower fields rising to the horizon, and we
were fifteen years younger, hoping to reach
St. Louis by nightfall. My wife beside me sang
as she took pictures. Her smile when she looked
over was the smile I saw now, back in Spain
again, passing melon and saffron fields, olive
groves, a ruined fortress slumped on a rise.
Road signs showed giant bulls and grain-grinding
wooden windmills from the world of Don Quixote.
Back to speed, we snacked on crackers and nuts
as the traffic thinned. Forgotten in a far corner
of the dashboard, silent and lost since we left
Oregon two days before, our portable satellite
navigator came to life and ordered us to turn right.
But we knew we should follow the road leading us
straight through the whitening afternoon light.

Late May in Zuheros, Andalucía

After his long walk uphill the old man
perches on a sun-soaked iron bench
in the Plaza de la Paz. He holds a sprig
of mint beneath his nose and allows
his eyes to close, his head with its burden
of thick white hair coming to rest
against the handle of his cane.

Nearby, where afternoon shadows
of a church and ruined castle meet,
four workers argue over plugged drains
as they scour the village fountain.

Roused by their laughter, the man slips
the mint behind his ear and rises,
keeping silent as he drifts by, smiling
with all he knows about preparing
for the season ahead. Before starting
back downhill, he stops to gaze a moment
at the olive farms in the hazy distance.

Spanish Edition

for Rebecca

The photojournalist tries to persuade
the author to sprawl across a sofa
in the lobby of a Madrid hotel and let
her long hair dangle like a fringed curtain
over a copy of her prizewinning book.
Then he tries to persuade her to stand
at the open window looking back at him
over one shoulder while her book rests
on the ledge. Maybe she could wink.
He turns in a circle and scans the space.
She should perch on the edge of a planter
under leaves dangling like a fringed curtain
over her book held flush to her heart.
Or she could hold two copies of her book,
one balanced in each hand like an offering
to the newspaper's readers eager to see
a side of her that no one has seen before.

First Night in London, 2012

From the dark back nook of a gluten-free
Italian restaurant in Waterloo,
dizzied by jet lag, full, we hear three
couples argue about exactly who
is to blame for the world economic
debacle. We can identify six
distinct accents but in each the same tone
when the word *America* is spoken.
Their crowded table shimmers in a cone
of light, strewn with lamb chops, olives, broken
loaves of rice-flour bread, a bowl of greens.
Across from each other, German and Greek
sharing fragments of gorgonzola cheese
lean together and shout: *Austerity!*
Stimulus! Holding hands, we rise to leave.
Weaving our way past them toward the street,
we are stopped near the bar where the waiter
ruefully gives us a torte to eat later.

Returning Home

I got up to see the river
shimmer in the full moon's light.
Something about the way current
and reflected clouds worked
on a shifting surface would tell me
for sure I was home and not still
in Spain. Lolling driftwood flickered
on the bank. Almost lost in shadow,
a sailboat rocked at anchor near
the island's north tip and from time
to time, because I knew they were
there, I saw the great blue heron
nests clustered at the treetops.
I thought if my body knew where
it was, sleep would come. But when
my wife called from bed I knew
I had gotten up only to return to her.

Sightings

I saw my brother in the sunstruck glass
of a nearby high-rise on the September
morning he would have turned seventy-two.
It was as though he had escaped the past
and all I could no longer remember.
I knew he was that flash of reflected light,
dazzling with life, in the same way I knew
he was the sudden gust of wind last night
that woke me as it spoke of things he did
not live to do. The waning summer moon
snagged in the river was him till he hid
from me behind the cloud that soon
gathered what glow remained. Wind-borne
songs he never heard reach me here,
dense with echoes of his raw baritone,
warmer than ever, unforgettably clear.

Today

Johnny is John now, and Billy is Bill.
Though I haven't seen them in fifty years
it feels like we're boys together still.
When his voice breaks, John's boyhood face appears
across the miles, and when Bill speaks of storms
we survived on our barrier island home
I forget and call him Billy, which makes
John gasp because it hurts so much to laugh.
The cancer has come back. He says it takes
all his strength some mornings just to take half
a breath, but then there might be a whole day
when he can almost forget, like today.

Turning Sixty-Five

Chicago, 2012

Late September mornings the lake whispers
winter to the edges of the harbor.
The whitecapped water churns silver and froths
at the breakwater. Within rising warmth
February is right there as wind gusting
against a shuttered beach house or the splash
of wetsuited swimmers along the boat line
parallel to shore, the clank of rigging.
A fisherman coughs and shrugs off his vest,
waiting to cast until we have cycled past.
When my wife coasts into the slow curve that takes
us west and slopes gently down to the heart
of the city, I follow, reading in her graceful
swerve the danger of wind-blown sand
mounded at the margin of the path.

Day's End

He keeps going back to the days of fat
cigars and belly laughs, short hair slicked down
by Vitalis, a double shot of Vat
69 in the club car. All around
his sickbed now, nurses and daughters prowl
through a glowing timeless space they call *Here*.
But he is gone again. Awake at owl
hour, he and the long-dead boys are out deer
hunting, out fishing for blues in Sheepshead
Bay. Then pinochle in the summer haze
as their boat rocks at anchor. They turn red
from hidden sun, watching the sea's soft grays
and blues fade even further at this day's
end when there is nothing left to be said.

Barrier Island

The carousel and bumper cars were long
gone. Seidel's Skee Ball, the five-cent fortune
telling machine, Izzy's Knishes, the shooting
gallery, teenage crooners harmonizing
at Waller's frozen custard stand: I saw
them all vanish when I was still a boy.
The three-story concrete watchtower
that protected us from Nazi submarines
was rubble. I played at dusk in the field
where it fell, walked beams of the bowling
alley that rose in its place. I was gone
myself before it became glass-faced condos
with a horizon view over flattened dunes,
before the storm took apart everything time
had left behind. On the news I saw a woman
walk where the boardwalk was now nothing
but pilings. The beach was scattered across
the island beneath the glare of morning sun.

NOTES

"October 30, 1938": On Halloween night—October 30, 1938—the *Mercury Theatre on the Air* broadcast Orson Welles's radio production of *The War of the Worlds*, a story of alien invasion originally published by H. G. Wells in 1898. Presented as though it were live, breaking news, *The War of the Worlds* fooled listeners into believing giant Martian creatures had landed in New Jersey and were slaughtering their way toward New York. According to the next day's *New York Times*, "a wave of mass hysteria seized thousands of radio listeners" and "disrupted households, interrupted religious services, created traffic jams and clogged communications systems."

"Crying over 'Scarlet Ribbons'": the popular song "Scarlet Ribbons (For Her Hair)" was written in 1949 by Evelyn Danzig and Jack Segal. It tells the story of a father desperate but unable—until a final miracle—to find the hair ribbons his daughter prays for. When I was young, I listened to the version sung by Harry Belafonte so many times that it became one of those brainworm tunes hooked in my memory. Hearing it again in my mid-sixties brought to mind a similar hair-accessory miracle I was lucky enough to experience when my daughter was young.

"Handel in London, 1741": George Frideric Handel's *Messiah* was composed in the summer of 1741, supposedly in a 24-day period, after he accepted an invitation from the Viceroy of Ireland to present a new oratorio. *Messiah*'s English-language text was cobbled together by Charles Jennens from passages in the King James Bible.

"Dylan Thomas at Sundown, November 9, 1953": Dylan Thomas died on November 9, 1953, at the age of thirty-nine.

"Samuel Beckett Throws Out the First Pitch": Samuel Beckett was an excellent cricket player as a young man. He appeared in two games for Dublin University, the only Nobel Prize–winning author to have played first-class cricket or to be featured in the *Wisden Cricketers' Almanack*. In August 1957 the Brooklyn Dodgers were owned by Walter O'Malley and were in their final weeks of existence before leaving the borough to become the Los Angeles Dodgers. Roy Campanella was their Hall of Fame catcher. Though they should have happened, the events in this poem are imaginary.

"Barrier Island": On October 29, 2012, Hurricane Sandy devastated the barrier island city of Long Beach, New York, where I lived between the ages of ten and eighteen.

CPSIA information can be obtained at www.ICGtesting.com
Printed in the USA
BVOW08s0317140915

417668BV00002B/21/P